Daddy

With Best Love

from

Eleanor Mary Teresa

Christmas 1949.

BRITAIN IN PICTURES
THE BRITISH PEOPLE IN PICTURES

ENGLISH ESSAYISTS

GENERAL EDITOR
W. J. TURNER

The Editor is most grateful to all those who have
so kindly helped in the selection of illustrations
especially to officials of the various public
Museums Libraries and Galleries and
to all others who have generously
allowed pictures and MSS
to be reproduced

ENGLISH ESSAYISTS

BONAMY DOBRÉE

*WITH
8 PLATES IN COLOUR
AND
23 ILLUSTRATIONS IN
BLACK & WHITE*

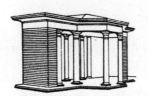

COLLINS · 14 ST. JAMES'S PLACE · LONDON
MCMXLVI

PRODUCED BY
ADPRINT LIMITED LONDON

PRINTED IN GREAT BRITAIN BY
CLARKE & SHERWELL LTD NORTHAMPTON
ON MELLOTEX BOOK PAPER MADE BY
TULLIS RUSSELL & CO LTD MARKINCH SCOTLAND

LIST OF ILLUSTRATIONS

PLATES IN COLOUR

BLACK AND WHITE ILLUSTRATIONS

ESSAYS OF SIR WILLIAM CORNWALLIS, 1632
Title page engraved by Thomas Cecill

INTRODUCTION

THOUGH the essay, a friendly, personal, informal piece of writing about anything you like, had existed from at least as early as the gay writings of Lucian in the second century B.C., the name in its everyday modern sense was first used when Montaigne published his *Essais* in 1580. Curious about the inner man, his purpose appeared to be no more than to give his friends a gossiping picture of his genial, sceptical mind ; and in the slippered ease of his retirement, he looked into himself

7

and wrote down what he found there. "I am myself the subject of my book," he told the reader, and he may have chosen the name to indicate that he was trying the thing out. His work was soon made current in English; so when in 1600 Sir William Cornwallis published *Essays*, he in his turn declared that he was engaged in finding out what he really thought, progressing towards the 'land of light' from the darkness of 'opinion.' "I write therefore for myself, and my self profits from my writing." The essay, you were led to believe, claimed to put aside all pedantry, all learning crammed out of books, and merely gave you the reasonable decent man talking to you or me or anyone else of what he thought about life : or rather, the man was talking to himself and allowing anyone who cared to do so to overhear him.

But Bacon, when he issued his first ten *Essays* in 1597, did something quite different. It appears that he copied out, and put into some sort of form, the aphorisms he had jotted down in his commonplace-book, reflections upon life that had come to him out of his own experience or from the heads of others, writers classical and modern alike, and from the Bible. He probably had in mind the little writings of the Latin authors, Cicero, and especially Seneca. So the self hardly comes in ; he is concerned with the world outside the individual ; he is positive, not sceptical or musing. You might, indeed, call these essays collections of philosophical "wise-cracks," based on learning and experience of the world.

Parallel with these, there developed a third kind of writing which we include among essays, disquisitions on a particular subject, one of the earliest of which, though not called an essay, is Sir Philip Sidney's *Apologie for Poetrie* (1595). It was the kind of literary discussion which later on Dryden called *An Essay of Dramatick Poesy* (1668), or Pope, writing in verse, called an *Essay on Criticism* (1711). We still call such writings essays when they deal with literary matters ; but works of philosophy or political learning such as Locke's *Essay Concerning Human Understanding* (1690) or Malthus's *Essay on the Principles of Population* (1798), we would not usually refer to as essays ; we would prefer to call them treatises.

So what we shall here discuss are the kind of writing called 'essays' by Montaigne and Bacon, such things as have appeared in magazines or journals ; or, where very early ones are concerned, would probably have appeared in magazines had they been invented ; or which might well have appeared in that way later on. All issue from Montaigne or Bacon ; some have more of the one in them, some more of the other. Some, like Lamb's, are purely and delightfully egotistical ; they spring from Montaigne. Others, such as Arnold's, try to arrive at some definite truth or principle ; they spring from Bacon. In nearly all there is a mixture ; there are few examples of a pure type. Indeed the essay is the most varied form of writing. It can be descriptive, moralistic, whimsical, exhorting or pleadingly self-revealing, critical or historical ; it can be anything you like. But all essays

Sir Philip Sidney, Author of *An Apologie for Poetrie*, 1595
Oil painting by an unknown artist

are aimed at the average reader, the 'common reader' to whom Virginia Woolf appealed in the essays she wrote under that title, though, like many of hers, they may be addressed to a reader assumed to be interested in a special subject. Essays, therefore, tend to be easy in style, and often they are deliberately familiar. There is something for everybody's palate in the rich array of English essays, something to pass away an idle moment, or something on which to spend three or four solid hours. They vary from the trivial to the portentous, from the wildly high-spirited to the gravely moral; at their most inconsequent they are idle amusement, at their best they are little gems of literature which give delight by their form, by what they have to tell us, and by the spirit they convey.

9

FRANCIS BACON, Lord Verulam (1561-1626) was primarily a philosopher, and it is to this rather than to his essays or his place in political history as Chancellor, that he owes his universal fame. So it is not surprising that his earliest essays are wholly aphoristic ; he is giving a picture not of himself, but of mankind. As he mellowed, however, and wrote more essays—they were added to in an edition of 1612, and reached the number of fifty-eight in his final edition of 1625—he came nearer the ordinary man because he talked of matters which interest the ordinary man. In one sense, certainly, his essays were still philosophical, but in them he was extending his scientific vision to include everyday affairs and the common emotions. In speaking of these, and of the things which happen to all men, he was filling the gap in his system ; he was intent "to pass from theological and philosophical truth to the truth of civil business," that is, to what you and I do. Therefore his style relaxes ; he becomes less stiffly formal. He seems just a little more to take you into his confidence, to be less concerned to make pronouncements, though it is still true, as has been well said, that "while Montaigne's chief concern is in a man sitting upon his 'owne taile,' Bacon's is a man sitting in an office chair." His personal likes and dislikes become visible, though they are veiled by his impersonal manner ; we know, because we feel, that much of what he writes comes out of his personal experience, is an expression of his own feeling. You see the difference if you compare his early and his late essays on Death. The first begins :

"Men fear death as children fear to go in the dark ; and as that natural fear in children is increased with tales, so is the other."

So it goes on, sprinkled with Latin quotations and examples drawn from the ancients, a discourse on a matter which scarcely affects him. But this is how his second essay begins :

"I have often thought about death, and I find it the least of all evils. All that which is past is as a dream ; and he that hopes or depends upon time coming, dreams waking."

Yet he doesn't pretend that others do not mind the idea of dying, and he goes on through a variegated catalogue of people who have reasons for fearing death, and in one passage at least forgets the office chair and becomes almost a poet :

"Death arrives gracious only to such as sit in darkness, or lie heavy burthened with grief and irons ; to the poor Christian that sits bound in the galley ; to despairful widows, pensive prisoners, and deposed kings ; to those whose fortune runs back, and whose spirits mutiny ; unto such death is a redeemer, and the grave a place for retiredness and rest.

"These wait upon the shore of death, and waft unto him to draw near, wishing above all others to see his star, that they might be led to his place ;

FRANCIS BACON, LORD VERULAM, 1561-1626
Frontispiece to W. Rawley's edition of Bacon's Works, 1638

wooing the remorseless sisters to wind down the watch of their life, and to break them off before the hour."

This essay is, one may think, his friendliest ; but he rarely appeals so directly to the emotions, preferring to keep his style matter-of-fact.

His essays have large titles : they are "Of Truth," "Of Envy," "Of Wisdom," and so on ; but his later ones are less abstract, dealing with such things as houses, gardens, the law, and a dozen matters of our daily lives, though sometimes they engage such abstract matters as, for instance,

"SEVEN OF THE CLOCKE"
Page from Nicolas Breton's *Fantastickes*, 1626

anger. The style is not difficult, but you must pay attention since his thought is very close-packed ; you cannot afford to miss anything. He is still popular, because, however aloof he may seem, he every now and then comes close to our own feelings : friendship "redoubleth joys, and cutteth griefs in halves : for there is no man that imparteth his joys to his friend, but he joyeth the more ; and no man that imparteth his griefs to his friend, but he grieveth the less." It must be confessed, however, that he is unduly hard on love !— though he is very wise on marriage, and on children and their education. As a good son of the Renaissance he believes in the greatness of man, saying in his essay "Of Parents and Children," "The perpetuity by generation is common to beasts ; but memory, merit, and noble works, are proper to men." You find that he does not care for self-seekers, men whose thoughts are always concerned for their own good, and he is sharp on them : "Wisdom for a man's self is, in many branches thereof, a depraved thing : it is the wisdom of rats, that will be sure to leave a house somewhat before it fall." He has no use for pedantry, for the pride of barren book-knowledge : "Studies serve for delight, for ornament, and for ability. . . . Crafty men contemn studies, simple men admire them, and wise men use them." And he adds, "Some books are to be tasted, others to be swallowed, and some few to be chewed and digested." His essays belong to the last class—"to be read wholly, and with diligence and attention." Then they become invigorating and delightful.

About the same time that Bacon was writing, two other popular forms made their appearance, forms which were later to become fused with the essay, to relieve its purely thoughtful content—a kind of yeast in the dough —and to make us look at our fellow-creatures. First we may take what we might call the 'descriptive piece,' sometimes combined with conversations and stories: we can take as a fair sample of this kind of writing the works of Nicolas Breton (1548? -1625?), who may have been a relation of Bacon's. Among his many entertaining works, the one which concerns us most here is his *Fantastics* (1626), which has descriptions of the seasons, the months, and the hours of the day. A very short one, "Seven of the Clock," will give an idea of what he was trying to do, namely to give you the feel of life at any particular time or season by describing what was going on, with all its variety of bustle and noise :

"It is now the seventh hour, and time begins to set the world hard to work : the milk-maids in their dairy to their butter and their cheese, the ploughmen to their ploughs and their harrows in

EARLY MORNING AT THE MARKET
Detail from the woodcut "Tittle-tattle," 1603

the field : the scholars to their lessons, the lawyers to their cases, the merchants to their accounts, shop-men to 'What lack you ?,' and every trade to his business. Oh 'tis a world to see how life leaps about the limbs of the healthful; none but finds something to do : the wise, to study, the strong, to labour : the Fantastic, to make love : the poet, to make verses : the player, to con his part : and the musician to try his note : every one in his quality, and according to his condition, sets himself to some exercise, either of the body, or the mind. And therefore since it is a time of much labour, and great use, I will thus briefly conclude of it : I hold it the enemy of idleness, and employer of industry. *Farewell*."

As Breton wrote them, such things are isolated pieces ; but they soon became absorbed in the body of the essay, merged in the general flow of consciousness of the reader. The other form which was to lend an enormous amount of colour to the essay was the 'character,' a form which goes back a long way in literary history, to Theophrastus, who lived about three

13

hundred years before Christ. Character writing was extremely popular in the early seventeenth century ; many poets and playwrights tried their hands at it (there were, for instance, the Overbury *Characters* of 1614, by Overbury, Webster and others) ; but the most famous collection is that of John Earle, (1601 ?-1665), later Bishop of Worcester and then of Salisbury, whose *Micro-cosmography, or a Piece of the World Discovered* was first published in 1628. He said that his characters were written "especially for his private recreation, to pass away the time in the country," and they read so easily that one may well believe this to be true. Earle amused himself by drawing spirited pen-pictures of a large number of such people as he met casually and could imagine more about : a grave divine, a drunkard, a reserved man, a shark, a plain country fellow, a pot-poet, a surgeon, a contemplative man, a she precise hypocrite, a cook. He wrote in short, sharp sentences, making types out of personalities. Here, for example, is part of "A Mere Alderman" :

"He is venerable in his gown, more in his beard, wherewith he sets not forth so much his own, as the face of a city. You must look on him as one of the town gates, and consider him not as a body, but a corporation."

All the time he displays a certain critical wit, which becomes tiring after a while, but is enlivening in small snatches. "A plain country fellow is one that manures his ground well, but lets himself lie fallow and untilled." It cannot be said that the future bishop was full of the milk of human kindness; most of his characters are satirically drawn, but sometimes he is more humane and tender :

"A good old man is the best of antiquity, and which we may with least vanity admire. . . . The next door of death sads him not, but he expects it calmly as his turn in Nature : and fears more his recoiling back to childishness than dust."

This sort of writing became a common part of the essay : Earle's figures are the ancestors of Sir Roger de Coverley, Will Wimble, and scores of others ; but the descendants came to be typical personalities rather than the abstract types the earlier writers aimed at presenting to the reader.

In the later half of the seventeenth century we find yet other elements creeping into the essay to give it its complete form ; or perhaps, not so much new elements as variants of older ones, made easier, more likeable, more friendly. Instead of the philosophic epigram we find musing contemplation; instead of a statement implying finality, we get discussion of a general idea. These two ingredients are best represented in the writings of Abraham Cowley (1618-1667) and of Sir William Temple (1628-1699). These new elements do not stand out clearly separated, as though the two writers were deliberately importing some new discovery, but they are mingled, seeming to enter in through a natural process of evolution. The essays of these two men approximate to the essay as we know it, but the form is not yet fully fleshed.

SIR WILLIAM TEMPLE, 1628-1699
Detail of an oil painting by Sir Peter Lely

Cowley's *Several Discourses by Way of Essays* (1668) seem very odd to us, being partly written in verse, and always concluding with poetry. Cowley is the intimate essayist again, nearer to Montaigne, to whom he sometimes refers, than he is to Bacon. He has nothing very new to say, but if his wisdom is largely drawn from the ancients, he divagates upon such stock themes as the deceit of ambition, the servitude of greatness and riches, and so on, with the conviction of a man who had been involved in great affairs, mixed with famous men, and had found that such a life was not one for him. They are personal, not abstract. He tells us in his "Essay of Myself" :

"I met with several great persons, whom I liked very well, but could not perceive that any part of their greatness was to be liked or desired, no more than I would be glad, or content to be in a storm, though I saw many ships which rid safely, and bravely in it. A storm would not agree with my stomach, if it did with my courage."

Thus when he writes so charmingly about the delight of gardens, one knows that he himself is a gardener, whereas one is pretty certain that Bacon had never plied a hoe. Moreover Cowley is such pleasant reading because wherever he can he uses the homely image ; he doesn't challenge your thought or argue with you, but makes you feel all the time how pleasant it is to agree with him, especially as he brings large ideas to the test of here and now. So he begins his essay on "The Shortness of Life" by asking :

"If you should see a man who were to cross from Dover to Calais, run about very busy and solicitous, and trouble himself many weeks before in making provisions for his voyage, would you commend him for a cautious and discreet person, or laugh at him for a timorous and impertinent coxcomb ?"

And he draws out the obvious moral without being portentous about it.

Cowley is, perhaps, our first really friendly essayist ; he never pretends to be more enlightened or more exquisite in feeling than the average man, and he asks you to share his shy and rather long-winded jokes :

"The best kind of glory, no doubt, is that which is reflected from honesty, as was the glory of Cato and Aristides, but it was harmful to them both, and is seldom beneficial to any man whilst he lives. What it is to him after his death I cannot say, because I love not philosophy merely notional and conjectural, and no man who has made the experiment has been so kind as to come back to inform us." ("Of Obscurity.")

Temple, on the other hand, was plainly fond of conjectural philosophy, and as a successful man of affairs who had been a great ambassador, liked to have notions about how things worked. Like Bacon, he attempted to bring the findings of philosophy and the discoveries of science into relation with life as we live it. Where Cowley tries to make you muse gently, Temple invites you to think rather more strenuously, about history, about Confucius, about civilisation generally : he liked the broad sweep, but he wrote for those who, as he did, judge a book for the pleasure it gives them rather than for the instruction it affords. Lamb called his style "plain natural chit chat, written in his elbow chair and undress." His gentle pessimism is attractive, best phrased perhaps at the conclusion of what is probably his best-known essay "Of Poetry," with which he brackets music ". . . Happy those that content themselves with these [pleasures], or any other so easy and so innocent ; and do not trouble the world, or other men, because they cannot be quiet themselves, though nobody hurts them ! When all is done, human life is, at the greatest and the best, but like a froward child, that must be played with and humoured a little to keep it quiet till it falls asleep, and then the care is over."

ABRAHAM COWLEY, 1618–1667
Miniature by Robert Flatman
By courtesy of Alan Evans, Esq.

JOSEPH ADDISON, 1672–1719
Oil painting by Sir Godfrey Kneller, painted for the Kit Cat Club, 1702–1717

TASTE, POLITENESS
AND TEA-TABLE PHILOSOPHY

THE writings of essayists, set down as they are for 'the common reader' necessarily reflect the sort of thing most people are thinking about. They are a kind of barometer of popular educated opinion and feeling. In the seventeenth century man was discovering himself, seeing himself, so to speak, in relation to the universe ; essays therefore tended to be philosophical. In the eighteenth, man thought he had settled the main philosophic questions, and left the great problems behind, so he began to work himself out as a social creature. The eighteenth century was creating the social man, that is, the man (and indeed, with increasing stress, the woman) who formed 'polite society,' and was to be full of the social virtues. Its essays, therefore, are nearly all moralistic.

That we are still under the influence of the eighteenth century is shown by the fact that there is a much more modern flavour about its writers than there is about those of the previous age. Their essays are more like ours. Yet it would be wrong to suppose that the form of the essay, say of Steele and Addison, was an inspired creation on their part. It had its forerunners, in, for instance, some of Defoe's writings ; and it mixed with the rather studious, retired manner of Temple, Cowley, Bacon or Montaigne, the rattling man-in-the-street attitude which had given zest to a good deal of writing from the days of Elizabeth (Nashe, Dekker and so on) to their own day (Tom Brown, Ned Ward and others), writing which was the vigorous, savoury, rough-and-tumble journalism of the past hundred and more years. Richard Steele (1672-1729) was a superb journalist, and when he produced *The Tatler*, which began in April 1709, he brought out something which immediately hit the taste of the day, that of a large new reading public, educated, and hungry for literature lighter than the theological polemics which still burdened the bookstalls, asking for easy reading which dealt in a cultivated way with what they were all thinking about. What he did, together with Joseph Addison (1672-1719) was to combine all the elements we have seen hitherto making up the essay, borrow a great deal from recent journalism, and present the world to itself as it knew itself. It was a magnificent invention, a triumph of journalistic genius.

Since *The Tatler* (it ran till January 1711), which was mainly Steele's, and *The Spectator* (March 1711 to December 1712) which was chiefly Addison's, were both newspapers, the essays had to be short, compact, and graceful. They had to be the sort of thing a man could pick up and read in the coffee-house while waiting for a friend, or when driving from one place to another ; or that a woman could read while her hair was being dressed, or toy with at the breakfast table. But however airy the writing might be, both men wanted to do two things ; first to civilise the large new

17

The TATLER.

By Isaac Bickerstaff Esq;

Quicquid agunt Homines nostri Farrago Libelli.

Tuesday, April 12. 1709.

THO' the other Papers which are publish'd for the Use of the good People of England have certainly very wholesom Effect; and are laudable in their particular Kinds, they do not seem to come up to the main Design of such Narrations, which, I humbly presume, should be principally intended for the Use of Politick Persons, who are so publick-spirited as to neglect their own Affairs to look into Transactions of State. Now these Gentlemen, for the most Part, being Persons of strong Zeal and weak Intellects, It is both a Charitable and Necessary Work to offer something, whereby such worthy and well-affected Members of the Commonwealth may be instructed, after their Reading, what to think: Which shall be the End and Purpose of this my Paper, wherein I shall from Time to Time Report and Consider all Matters of what Kind soever that shall occur to Me, and publish such my Advices and Reflections every Tuesday, Thursday, and Saturday, in the Week, for the Convenience of the Post. It is also resolv'd by me to have something which may be of Entertainment to the Fair Sex, in Honour of whom I have taken the Title of this Paper. I therefore earnestly desire all Persons, without Distinction, to take it in for the present Gratis, and hereafter at the Price of one Penny, forbidding all Hawkers to take more for it at their Peril. And I desire all Persons to consider, that I am at a very great Charge for proper Materials for this Work, as well as that before I resolv'd upon it, I had settled a Correspondence in all Parts of the Known and Knowing World ; and forasmuch as this Globe is not trodden upon by mere Drudges of Business only, but that Men of Spirit and Genius are justly to be esteem'd as considerable Agents in it, we shall not upon a Dearth of News present you with musty Foreign Edicts, or dull Proclamations, but shall divide our Relation of the Passages which occur in Action or Discourse throughout this Town, as well as elsewhere, under such Dates of Places as may prepare you for the Matter you are to expect, in the following Manner :

All Accounts of Gallantry, Pleasure, and Entertainment, shall be under the Article of White's Chocolate-house ; Poetry, under that of Will's Coffee-house ; Learning, under the Title of Grecian ; Foreign and Domestick News, you will have from St. James's Coffee-house ; and what else I shall on any other Subject offer, shall be dated from my own Apartment.

I once more desire my Reader to consider, That as I cannot keep an Ingenious Man to go daily to Will's, under Two-peace each Day merely for his Charges ; to White's, under Sixpence ; nor to the Grecian, without allowing him some Plain Spanish, to be as able as others at the Learned Table ; and that a good Observer cannot speak with even Kidney at St. James's without clean Linnen. I say, these Considerations will, I hope, make all Persons willing to comply with my Humble Request (when my Gratis Stock is exhausted) of a Penny a Piece ; especially since they are sure of some Proper Amusement, and that it is impossible for me to want Means to entertain 'em, having, besides the Helps of my own Parts, the Power of Divination, and that I can, by casting a Figure, tell you all that will happen before it comes to pass.

But this last Faculty I shall use very sparingly, and not speak of any Thing 'till it is pass'd, for fear of divulging Matters which may offend our Superiors.

White's Chocolate-House, April 7.

THE deplorable Condition of a very pretty Gentleman, who walks here at the Hours when Men of Quality first appear, is what is very much lamented. His History is, That on the 9th of September, 1705. being in his One and twentieth Year, he was washing his Teeth at a Tavern Window in Pall-Mall, when a fine Equipage pass'd by, and in it a young Lady who look'd up at him ; away goes the Coach, and the young Gentleman pull'd off his Night-Cap, and instead of rubbing his Gums, as he ought to do, out of the Window 'till about Four a Clock, he sits him down, and spoke not a Word 'till Twelve at Night ; after which, he began to enquire, If any Body knew the Lady... The Company ask'd, What Lady? But he said no more, 'till they broke up at Six in the Morning. All the ensuing Winter he went from Church to Church every Sunday, and from Play-house to Play-house all the Week, but could never find the Original of the Picture which dwelt in his Bosom. In a Word, his Attention to any Thing, but his Passion, was utterly gone. He has lost all the Money he ever play'd for, and been confuted in every Argument he has enter'd upon since the Moment he first saw her. He is of a Noble Family, has naturally a very good Air, is of a frank, honest Temper : But this Passion has so extreamly maul'd him, that his Features are set and uninform'd, and his whole Visage is deaden'd by a long Absence of Thought. He never appears in any Alacrity, but when rais'd by Wine ; at which Time he is sure to come hither, and throw away a great deal of Wit on Fellows, who have no Sense further than just to observe, That our poor Lover has most Understanding

THE FIRST NUMBER OF "THE TATLER"

EIGHTEENTH CENTURY LONDON
Detail of an aquatint by F. Jukes after W. Moss, 1774

middle-class which had lately come into being ; and secondly, Addison especially, to stop people from eternally talking politics at a time when politics were becoming alarmingly bitter. They did not want to aim either too high or too low, and luckily both of them were masters of the middle style.

There is more zest about Steele's writing, as there was about the man ; you feel that he got enormous fun out of it all. It was he who invented the whole thing, the pretending to write from different places (though Defoe had invented The Scandal Club in his *Review*), and the mock letters ; Sir Roger de Coverley came first from his hand. He enjoyed every line of it, the creation and the moralising together. "I must confess," he wrote in the last *Tatler*, "it has been a most exquisite pleasure to me to frame characters of domestic life, and put those parts of it which are least observed into an agreeable view ; to inquire into the seeds of vanity and affection, to lay before the readers the emptiness of ambition : in a word, to trace human life through all its mazes and recesses, and show much shorter methods than men ordinarily practise to be happy, agreeable, and great."

19

We suspect that what gave him the most pleasure was the invention.

Look at him at work on Sir Roger, an immortal creation, the old-fashioned shrewd, blunt, kindly, honest, simple-minded even rather stupid country squire :

"It is said he keeps himself a bachelor by reason he was crossed in love by a perverse beautiful widow of the next county to him. Before his disappointment Sir Roger was what you call a fine gentleman, had often supped with my Lord Rochester and Sir George Etherege [wits and rakes of Charles II's day], fought a duel upon his first coming to town, and kicked Bully Dawson in a public coffee-house for calling him youngster. But being ill-used by the above-mentioned widow, he was very serious for a year and a half ; and though, his temper being naturally jovial, he at last got over it, he grew careless of himself, and never dressed afterwards . . . He is now in his fifty-sixth year, cheerful, gay, and hearty ; . . . all the young women profess love to him, and the young men are glad of his company. When he comes into a house he calls the servants by their names, and talks all the way upstairs to a visit." (*Spectator* 2.)

What could be more homely, more life-like, more familiar than that ? —and so with the rest of the Club, Will Wimble, Sir Andrew Freeport and the others, each of them in their way observed individuals, but rather more the old 'character' come to life.

Addison, it must be regretfully confessed, was the greater writer of the two (though some, with Landor, may prefer Steele's prose as being cleaner-cut) ; regretfully, because he was undoubtedly something of a prig. In the tenth *Spectator* he tells us what his object in writing was, and we may compare it with what Steele had felt about *The Tatler*.

"It was said of Socrates, that he brought philosophy down from heaven to inhabit among men ; and I shall be ambitious to have it said of me, that I have brought philosophy out of closets and libraries, schools and colleges, to dwell in clubs and assemblies, at tea-tables and in coffee-houses."

And what was more, he even, in a sense, managed to do so, a fact which compels our admiration even if to-day we find his philosophy a little disagreeable. If he was forever dwelling upon morals he did it very urbanely; and if there is now and then a hint of the parson, his humour lightens it all. He made even his condescension to the 'fair sex' palatable to his day, however insufferable it may seem to us as coming from someone who knows himself to be a superior person. And if he was for goodness he was also for gaiety, and constantly made fun of solemn or lugubrious piety. The interesting thing is that these essays with a purpose which was so obvious were yet so greatly relished : it is explained by the fact that both Steele and Addison made follies and extravagances so gently ridiculous that everybody could take them good-humouredly and apply the moral to their friends without malice. There is no doubt that the two collaborators did a a great deal to make society better ; and society loved them for it. They

1748 Aug:
1 Dr. Johnson
2 Bp. of Salisbury
3 Ld. Harcourt
4 Mr. Cibber
5 Mr. Garrick
6 Mrs. Trale
7 Mr. Nash.
8 Miss Chudleigh.
9 Mr. Pitt
10 A. O. Esqr
11 Ld. Powis
12 Dutchess of Norfolk
13 Miss Banks.
14 Lady Lincoln
15 Mrs. Little
16 The Baron
17 Anonym
18 Mrs. Onslow
19 Miss Onslow
20 Mrs. Johnson
21 Mr. Whiston

DR. JOHNSON AT TUNBRIDGE WELLS IN 1748
Engraving from Boswell's *Life of Johnson*

imparted a great deal of learning, but they were never pedantic. They used all the devices the earlier essayists had taught them—the philosophic thought, the description, the character, and so on, and they developed and welded them together till their volumes seem half-way to the novel, especially since they brought their philosophic thoughts close to the life that everybody knew. Also, they enlarged the imagination. The range covered is amazing ; from hen-pecked husbands to idolatry, from a grinning-match to the sublimities of Milton, from lap-dogs to the Vision of Mirza, from French frivolity to the meaning of tragedy. There were allegories and stories, descriptions of people, imaginary letters, discussions of the ballads : wit enlivened morality, and gentle satire gave a spice to serious reproof.

It was extremely well done ; and if to us now the prose seems a little monotonous—especially Addison's—the morality insipid, the patronage of women infuriating ; if the general self-righteousness makes us feel explosive ; and if we feel that Addison exhibited with pride all the worst Victorian virtues (thus later plunging Macaulay into lachrymose ecstasies), there is still something about the essays which attracts us as we read them, and this something is the valiant attempt to see all behaviour as a whole, to make man into a civilised creature. And after all, the prose is first-rate prose of its kind, the ideal a civilised ideal—even a little too civilised :

"There are many more shining qualities in the mind of man, but there is none so useful as discretion ; it is this indeed which gives value to all the rest, which sets them at work in their proper times and places, and turns them to the advantage of the person who is possessed of them. Without it learning is pedantry, and wit impertinence ; virtue itself looks like weakness ; the best parts only qualify a man to be sprightly in errors, and active to his own prejudice." (*Spectator* 225.)

That sort of admonition was necessary in a turbulent, faction-riven age, such as that of Queen Anne ; and however much we may feel that Addison talks down to us, he was a masterly populariser of the thought of his day, in philosophy, in morals, in religion, in politics : and the way we think about many matters now is still largely thanks to him.

Dr. Samuel Johnson (1709-1784) was, as we all know, a more portentous figure : he was the Grand Cham of literature, and he didn't persuade you ; he just told you. There was no arguing with him. But he did it in such a bluff way, appealing to you as the sensible fellow that you really are, that nobody could take offence. He is never the 'superior person' that Addison was: he never talks down to you. You may not always agree with him, but you can't help feeling that he is wise. He makes up his sentences and uses his words in such a way that they come down with a thump of finality : you have to summon up all your courage to disagree with him.

His best-known journalistic essays are those he printed in *The Rambler* (1750-1752), a periodical written almost entirely by himself ; and *The Idler* papers he wrote for *The Universal Chronicle or Weekly Gazette* between April 1758 and April 1760. He also wrote for Hawkesworth's *Adventure*, and for *The Gentleman's Magazine*, the last being the most successful of all magazines, and the first to have that name. It began in 1731 as a kind of '*Reader's Digest*,' but changing its character, largely on the advice of Johnson, who wrote Parliamentary reports for it, it ran as a generally informative and essay journal till 1868. (A 'completely new series' ran from 1868 to 1907.) Johnson's prefaces to an edition of the poets (1779-1781), later collected as *The Lives of the Poets*, can also be regarded as biographical and critical essays, as can his preface to his edition of Shakespeare (1765). Though in these also he displays his qualities—he is never trite or provincial as Addison often is—it is with *The Rambler* and *The Idler* that we shall be concerned.

Johnson used all the methods Addison had used before him, the straightforward disquisition, the letter, the oriental or other tale, the examples from ancient times, the character, and the description of a scene. He covered much the same ground, morals, religion, criticism ; but he is profounder, more deeply moved, and he accepts human nature for what it is. Take this : he is not preaching tolerance and understanding, he is exhibiting them, not without humour :

"I am afraid there is little hope of persuading the young and sprightly part of my readers, upon whom the spring naturally forces my attention, to learn from the great process of nature the difference between diligence and hurry, between speed and precipitation; to prosecute their designs with calmness, to watch the concurrence of opportunity, and endeavour to find the lucky moment which they cannot make. Youth is the time of enterprise and hope ; having yet no occasion of comparing one force with any opposing power, we naturally form presumptions in our own favour, and imagine that obstruction and impediment will give way before us. The first repulses rather inflame vehemence than teach prudence : a brave and generous mind is long before it suspects its own weakness, or submits to sap the difficulties which it expected to subdue by storm. . ." (*Rambler* III.)

THE
RAMBLER.

Numb. 1.   Price 2 *d.*

TUESDAY, *March* 20, 1749-50.

To be continued on Tuesdays *and* Saturdays.

Cur tamen hoc libeat potiùs decurrere campo,
Per quèm magnus equos Auruncæ flexit Alumnus,
Si vacat, et placidi rationem admittitis, edam.

                                        Juv.

THE Difficulty of the first Address, on any new Occasion, is felt by every Man in his Transactions with the World, and confessed by the settled and regular Forms of Salutation, which Necessity has introduced into all Languages. Judgment was wearied with the inextricable Perplexity of being forced upon Choice, where there was often no Motive to Preference ; and it was found convenient that some easy Method of Introduction should be established, which, if it wanted the Allurement of Novelty, might enjoy in its place the Security of Prescription.

Perhaps few Authors have presented themselves before the Publick, without wishing that such ceremonial Modes
                                                    of

THE FIRST NUMBER OF "THE RAMBLER"
Published Tuesday, March 20th, 1749-50

23

Johnson—in common with the scores of other writers who contributed to the hundred odd periodicals that ran in the eighteenth century—would never have written as he did but for *The Tatler*, *The Spectator* and the other journals produced by Steele and Addison ; but he brought something individual, as the others did in varying degrees. In *The Rambler* he used all his heavy artillery, but *The Idler* is a good deal lighter : instructive entertainment takes the place of entertaining instruction. The latter paper deals much with idle people, the most famous of whom are Mr. Sober, perhaps a castigation of himself in his weaker moments; and Dick Minim, the critic. Dick knows nothing at first hand, but sets himself up as an authority on the strength of picking up all the accepted opinions, and quoting the great critics of the past, whom he by no means understands. The type is with us yet, and Dick Minim can still amuse us as the portrait of a contemporary. Throughout, Johnson, like his immediate forerunners, is a moralist, but he is sterner than they are. While Addison's standard was the social one, Johnson's was the ethical one, with the result that he seems less out of date, since manners change more than ethics do. Like Bacon, he challenges us to thought, and to read him is to be stimulated.

Oliver Goldsmith (1730-1774), though a friend of Johnson's, wrote in a very different style. If Johnson stood plumb in front of the fire and talked at you, Goldsmith sat in the ingle and talked with you, while he sipped his hot drink. He wrote for many periodicals, such as Smollett's *British Magazine*, but especially for his own short-lived paper *The Bee* (October, November 1759). He also wrote for the *Public Ledger*, in which appeared his 'Chinese Letters,' published in 1762 as *The Citizen of the World*. The letters purport to be those of a Chinaman visiting England, giving to his compatriots his impressions of this strange European civilisation in which he finds himself. The effect Goldsmith aimed at was one of gentle, humorous satire. All our assumptions, actions and customs are looked at from a slightly odd angle, with the result that most of our accepted habits, even our most solemn doings, are made to look faintly ludicrous. The tone is given by Lien Chi Altingi writing to his friend :

"When I survey the absurdities and falsehoods with which the books of Europeans are filled, I thank Heaven for having been born in China, and that I have sagacity enough to detect imposture." (Letter xvi.)

Thus when we read these letters, we think them extremely funny, but feel them to be uncomfortably shrewd. So many of the things we take for granted are made to look delightfully absurd. In their way these essays are the most charming that had been produced ; though they are in a sense moral—if to look at one's self clearly is the essential step in morality— they are entirely free from the flavour of moralising ; we never feel we are being whipped, goaded, or enticed into virtue. They make us look upon life with an alert, amused, and tolerantly critical eye.

SIR RICHARD STEELE, 1672–1729
Oil painting by Sir Godfrey Kneller, painted for the Kit Cat Club, 1702–1717

WILLIAM HAZLITT, 1778–1830
Miniature by John Hazlitt, 1791
By courtesy of the Committee of the Maidstone Museum

BY the third quarter of the eighteenth century, the essay had become a natural mode of communication, as befits a civilised age where real conversation, not the yaffle of the club-room or the tattle of the drawing-room, sets the tone. From now on it tended to be lighter, more personal, the idea of its functions being widely accepted ; thus Bacon was giving place to Montaigne. But though there was a continual flow of excellent writers, not at all dull or bad reading, there was no outstanding figure till we come to the nineteenth century, to that group which contains the names of Coleridge, Lamb, Hazlitt and De Quincey—together with those there is no space to enlarge upon—a group individually very various, but which represents a distinct stage. They are not moralistic in the obvious sense, so much as literary-philosophical, and again suddenly seem much closer to us than the eighteenth century essayists.

Man was getting tired of considering himself as a social creature only, and was trying to rediscover himself as an individual, whose interest for others, as well as for himself, lay precisely in his being different from other people.

Samuel Taylor Coleridge (1772-1834) is the most deeply philosophical, and in *The Friend* (1809 ; published as a book in 1818) we find the ethical and literary ideas which form part of the stock which give him his high position as thinker and critic of fundamental notions. And however much he may be based on the eighteenth, and indeed the seventeenth century, his political statements still strike home (since they really are fundamental), and the following passage might have been written in say, 1938, as justly as during the war in the middle of which he was writing :

"Little prospective wisdom can that man obtain, who hurrying onward with the current, or rather torrent, of events, feels no interest in their importance, except as far as his curiosity is excited by their novelty, and to whom all reflection and retrospect are wearisome. If ever there were a time when the formation of just public principles becomes a duty of private morality ; when the principles of morality in general ought to be made to bear on our public suffrages, and to affect every great national determination; when, in short, his country should have a place by every Englishman's fireside ; and when the feelings and truths which give dignity to the fireside and tranquillity to the deathbed, ought to be present and influensive in the cabinet and in the senate—that time is now with us." (*The Friend* I. 10.)

And who would say that the comment is not relevant now !

It is, however, Charles Lamb (1775-1834) who is the best known and best loved of this group, and who has had the widest influence on the essay. His famous *Essays of Elia* first appeared in *The London Magazine* from 1820 to 1823, a second series coming out some ten years later. It is the fashion nowadays to decry Lamb as being too mannered, too fanciful, altogether too egotistical and whimsical : but that is largely because his imitators—and people still imitate Lamb—have imitated the wrong thing. Imitators usually do. Because of his way of writing, a theory has grown up that the less an essay is 'about' the more perfect it is ; the theory is a forcing to absurdity of the Montaigne position. Lamb's essays, nevertheless, are very definitely about something other than himself, though he seems always to be writing about himself alone. If one wanted to make a contrast between him and the usual run of eighteenth century essayists, one would say that whereas they were moralists, he was impressionistic ; indeed he goes back further, and his style is Temple's rather than Addison's, though he has a literary sense and tact unknown to the retired ambassador.

He is egotistic in the sense that rather than seem to be uttering great truths about things, he gives his own feelings about them, and in the main he treats of small things (which after all make up most of our lives), preferring, as Hazlitt said of him, byeways to highways. But out of these small things he developed thoughts which spread over the whole of a personal life. Great issues do not figure in his titles; one is invited to read, rather, on subjects such as roast pig, or chimney sweepers, or Mrs. Battle's opinions on whist, but what you find implicit in what follows is an attitude towards life. He is at his best when he is reminiscent, while much of his writing is pervaded by a tenderness towards the helpless, the weak, or the oppressed, a tenderness which some find sentimental, but which, all the same, is invariably controlled. Steeped as he was in seventeenth century literature, he loved the strange striking word so much that its use almost became a vice with him. Yet how apt it seems, how it gives just that turn of whimsicality which is a defence against sentimentality, a whimsicality which it must be confessed itself sometimes came perilously near to being a vice. Yet look at the word 'nigritude' in the opening paragraph of his "In Praise of Chimney-Sweepers" :

A Young Chimney Sweep
Coloured aquatint by William Craig
From "Cries of London," 1804

26

Coleridge.   *Mary Lamb.*   *Cha' Lamb.*   *Southey.*   *Wordsworth.*   *W. Blake.*   *Flaxman.*

A GROUP OF LITERARY FIGURES IN THE EARLY NINETEENTH CENTURY
Detail from a lithograph after a fresco by E. Armitage

"I like to meet a sweep—understand me—not a grown sweeper—old chimney-sweepers are by no means attractive—but one of those tender novices, blooming through their first nigritude, the maternal washings not quite effaced from the cheek. . . ."

Similar effects crop up everywhere.

But whatever archaic mannerisms (sometimes friendly parodies), or irrelevant eccentricities may here and there a little irritate you in Lamb, he is among the most intimate of our essayists ; he really is like Montaigne. Although he was the close companion of the greatest literary figures of his day, we never feel as we read him that he is anything but a lovable ordinary man, lovable because he appreciates our actions, understands our feelings. In talking about "New Year's Eve," he tells us how he does not want to leave this life because "a new state of being staggers me," and : "Sun, and sky, and breeze, and solitary walks, and summer holidays, and the greenness of fields, and the delicious juices of meats and fishes, and society, and the cheerful glass, and candle-light, and fireside conversations, and innocent vanities, and jests, and *irony itself*—do these things go out with life ?

"Can a ghost laugh, or shake his gaunt sides, when you are pleasant with him ?

27

"And you, my midnight darlings, my Folios ; must I part with the intense delight of having you (huge armfuls) in my embraces ? Must knowledge come to me, if it come at all, by some awkward experiment of intuition, and no longer by the familiar process of reading ?

"Shall I enjoy friendships there, wanting the smiling indications which point me to them here—the recognisable face—the 'sweet assurance of a look'?"

As compared with his predecessors, with him we feel delightfully free of what he called the perpetual coxcombry of our moral pretensions.

Not that Lamb was always personal ; his critical essays reach out beyond his own affairs, memories, and idiosyncrasies, to general principles, which are based, as all good criticism ultimately is, on what he feels he knows in his bones to be good. The essay on "The Artificial Comedy of the Last Century" was a landmark in the criticism of Restoration Comedy, for though its argument is false, it is freshly thought and eagerly argued. Perhaps Lamb is the sort of writer you either warm to very much, or ought to leave severely alone.

Owning some affinities with Lamb, whose portrait he painted, is William Hazlitt (1778-1830). Bagehot thought him the better essayist. He is to some degree a personal writer, whose subject is himself, but he is something of a bully to his reader, and is occasionally bad-tempered. He wrote for many reviews, including the *Edinburgh*—of which more later—on all sorts of subjects, but his critical work is in many respects his best. He had a fine, clear, direct style, corresponding with a fine, clear, direct head, and he wrote memorably. One does not forget the portrait of Wordsworth in "My First Acquaintance with Poets," nor that of Jeremy Bentham in *The Spirit of the Age* (1825). He wrote also on more general subjects than Lamb was inclined to do, as a glance at the essays in *Winterslow* (posthumous) or *Table Talk, or Original Essays on Men and Manners* (1821-1822) will show, and he had a similar passion for the Elizabethan dramatists. Yet by way of embarking on a general disquisition he will often tell you of himself. Thus he begins "On Consistency of Opinion" with "Many people boast of being masters in their own house. I pretend to be master in my own mind." But equally often he shoots straight away at his target, as in "On Party Spirit" :

"Party spirit is one of the *profoundnesses of Satan*, or, in modern language one of the dexterous *equivoques* and contrivances of our self-love, to prove that we, and those who agree with us, combine all that is excellent and praiseworthy in our own persons (as in a ring-fence), and that all the vices and deformity of human nature take refuge in those that differ from us." (*Winterslow* III.)

He can be scathing enough to make us look pretty closely into ourselves, as, in the same essay, "We may be intolerant even in advocating the cause of toleration, and so bent on making proselytes to freethinking as to allow

CHARLES LAMB, 1775-1834
Detail of an oil painting by William Hazlitt, 1804

no one to think freely but ourselves." Hazlitt was a widely read, widely thoughtful man, vigorous, combative, generous where he felt generosity was called for, biting where he thought reproof was needed.

Perhaps no short passage can give his quality better than the conclusion of a slashing attack on Byron in *The Spirit of the Age*, a collection consisting mainly of articles contributed to *The New Monthly Magazine*:

"We had written thus far when news came of the death of Lord Byron, and put an end at once to a strain of somewhat peevish invective, which was intended to meet his eye, not to insult his memory. Had we known that we were writing his epitaph, we must have done it with a different feeling. As it is, we must think it better, and more like himself, to let what we had written stand, than to take up our leaden shafts, and try to melt them into 'tears of sensibility', or mould them into dull praise and an affected show of candour. We were not silent during the author's lifetime, either for his reproof or encouragement (such as we could give, and *he* did not disdain to accept), nor can we now turn undertaker's men to fix the glittering plate upon his coffin, or fall into the procession of popular woe. Death cancels everything but truth, and strips a man of everything but genius and virtue. It is a sort of natural canonization. It makes the meanest of us sacred ; it installs the poet in his immortality, and lifts him to the skies. Death is the great assayer of the sterling ore of talent. . . . We consign the least worthy qualities to oblivion, and cherish the nobler and imperishable nature with double pride and fondness. . . ."

In spite of his familiarity he belongs to the Baconian rather than to the Montaigne family, arriving at a generalisation by applying hard thinking to every day, and in such a way that to read him is invigorating. One cannot rise from an essay of his without having thought about one's own self : when he is amusing, as he often is, it is not seldom at our own expense. Yet he is never dully moral ; he does not ask you to fit yourself into a social scheme, to make yourself conform : you are for him an individual. To read him, then, is like bathing in the sea on a fine clear sunny day ; but the water is cold, even a little rough : and there is plenty of salt in it.

If Coleridge is the profoundest of this group, Lamb the most intimate, and Hazlitt the most invigorating, Thomas De Quincey (1785-1859) is the most imaginative. He does not play delightedly with words as Lamb does, nor shoot them at you as Hazlitt is too often inclined to do ; he satisfies you with them by means of an extraordinary music. Extremely learned in the more mysterious kinds of lore, which seems to have imbued his opium dreams, there is nearly always something a little startlingly fantastic about De Quincey. The obvious illustration is the most famous of his essays, "Murder Considered as one of the Fine Arts." (*Blackwood's* 1827). His criticism is not that of a man of letters, a man who knows the craft, so much as of an artist, intensely sensitive to what the work of art he is experiencing is doing to him. So he sees things that others do not see, and we may take as example the deeply probing little essay on "The Knocking at the Gate in Macbeth." But his most personal things are still his opium-haunted musings, such as "Levana, and Our Ladies of Sorrow," and one may extract a passage full of sonorities and enchanting modulations :

"The second sister is called *Mater Suspiriorum*—Our Lady of Sighs. She never scales the clouds, nor walks abroad upon the winds. She wears no diadem. And her eyes, if they were ever seen, would be neither sweet nor subtle ; no man could read their story ; they would be found filled with perishing dreams, and with wrecks of forgotten delirium. But she raises not her eyes ; her head, on which sits a dilapidated turban, droops for ever, for ever fastens on the dust. She weeps not. She groans not. But she sighs inaudibly at intervals. Her sister Madonna [Our Lady of Tears]

THOMAS DE QUINCEY, 1785-1859
Detail of a chalk drawing by J. Archer, 1855

is oftentimes stormy and frantic, raging in the highest against heaven, and demanding back her darlings. But Our Lady of Sighs never clamours, never defies, dreams not of rebellious aspirations. She is humble to abjectness. Hers is the meekness that belongs to the hopeless. Murmur she may, but it is in her sleep. Whisper she may, but it is to herself in the twilight. Mutter she does at times, but it is in solitary places that are desolate as she is desolate, in ruined cities, and when the sun has gone down to his rest."

But even in De Quincey's lifetime, this delicate wind-music was to give place to noisier instruments, to the drum, the trumpet, and the cymbal.

31

THE *Edinburgh Review* (1802-1829) has already been mentioned, and with its name should be coupled that of *Blackwood's Magazine*, once familiarly known as 'Maga,' begun in 1817 as a rather lighter-weight rival of the *Edinburgh*, and still shyly running. Most of the great essayists of the first half of last century wrote for one or the other, according to their politics or literary affiliations. The *Edinburgh* was Whig, and handled the Lake poets roughly; 'Maga' was Tory, and trounced "the cockney school" (Lamb, Hazlitt, Keats, etc.). If these reviews were rough and often unjust, they certainly raised the standard of criticism and literary appreciation. They went at it hammer and tongs, they employed the best pens, and what they said mattered. We are approaching the brief, happy time from about 1830 to 1880 when the nation took its literature seriously, and the great magazines were a social and literary force conscious of their responsibility. Bagehot said of Lord Jeffrey, the most famous editor of the *Edinburgh*, that "he invented the trade of editorship. Before him an editor was a bookseller's drudge; he is now a distinguished functionary."

The most glittering figure, the man who owed most to this form of publication, and to whom in turn the *Edinburgh* owed greatly increased sales, was certainly Thomas Babington Macaulay (1800-1859). Most of the essays, first collected in 1843, appeared in this magazine, though many well-known ones were written as articles in the *Encyclopaedia Britannica*. He never wrote on trivial, personal, or imaginative subjects, but always on great figures or historical subjects, in which his astonishing memory (perhaps the cause of his 'inexperiencing mind'), and his first-hand acquaintance with matters of state, gave him that abounding certainty which is characteristic of his writing. He was never in doubt about anything; he felt that he was uttering unassailable truths; so his essays have every mark of impersonality. However much you may be opposed to his view, he is irresistibly readable : to embark on one of his essays is like stepping into a powerful car which rushes you along helplessly, to the regular throb of the relentless pistons of his prose. He never lets you off anything, never suggests; he tells you all. His blacks are blacks and his whites are Whigs, and all is judged by that touchstone. You will learn a lot from Macaulay, but a deal of what you learn will be wrong. Yet it will all be worth reading, however lengthy, even the essay on Warren Hastings, which is about three times as long as this book. His digressions themselves often fill more pages than a whole essay in *The Spectator*, they are always full of meat, astonishingly alive, and all contribute to the main effect, the patent intention, which is to make you know—or think you know—all that anyone would expect you to be conversant with. A short extract from the essay on Sir William Temple will serve as an illustration. Macaulay is describing how France had re-

THE DEATH OF CLORINDA

Oil painting by William Hazlitt, 1802, after a painting by Lodovico Lana in the Louvre

THE TOWN OF ITRI, SOUTH ITALY

Pencil, pen and wash drawing by John Ruskin, 1819–1900

placed Spain as the threatening despot of Europe, as a preface to something Temple was to do :

". . .The sceptre had passed away from Spain. That mighty empire, on which the sun never set, which had crushed the liberties of Italy and Germany, which had occupied Paris with its armies, and covered the British seas with its sails, was at the mercy of every spoiler ; and Europe observed with dismay the rapid growth of a new and formidable power. Men looked at Spain and saw only weakness disguised and increased by pride, dominions of vast bulk and little strength, tempting, unwieldy, and defenceless, an empty treasury, a sullen and torpid nation, a child on the throne, factions in the council, ministers who served only themselves, and soldiers who were terrible only to their countrymen."

There seems to be no need to enquire any further.

But the object of the writers in the group which follows was to urge their readers all the time to enquire further. The essay was entering on a different phase. If the earliest essayists invited you to think for thinking's sake ; if those of the eighteenth century advised you to think so as to become a good social individual ; if the group we have just been considering asked you to look at the queerness of man, this new generation urged, implored, or lured you to think as a responsible member of society, responsible not only for yourself but for the whole of the community. If for Macaulay—whom one can group among the discoverers of man as a unique creature only because he felt that he was the type of all reasonable men—the world was the best of all possible worlds, or at any rate would be in a generation or two, for this group England at least was hideous and ignoble, and they believed that something should be done about it by their readers.

Thomas Carlyle (1795-1881) was the most vociferous of them all. He hated what was going on in the world, and the philosophy which allowed, indeed encouraged, the way things were happening. The Calvinistic peasant of Ecclefechan wrote feverishly for years in his "Babylonish dialect," which seems to hurl you about as you read. His intuitions as regards the evil were right, but his hatred of progress and parliaments, of anything which he called 'unveracious' (that is, anything he disapproved of), made him preach the absurdity of a return to the middle ages, combined with a form of dictatorship. This belief he expounded, and pounded away at, half a life-time, in *Sartor Resartus* (1833-4, essays in *Fraser's Magazine*), *Chartism* (1839), *Heroes and Hero-Worship* (1841, a series of lectures), and *Latter-Day Pamphlets* (1843), and to the end. You might be fiercely indignant at what he said, but he was so forceful, so vivid, so picturesque, in fact so much the artist, that you could not in those days resist reading him ; and even now it is hard to put him down if you have once taken him up.

". . . Let inventive men consider, whether the Secret of the Universe, and of Man's life there, does, after all, as we rashly fancy it, consist in making money ? There is One God, just, supreme, almighty ; but is

Mammon the name of him ?—With a Hell which means 'Failing to make money' I do not think there is any Heaven possible which would suit one well ; not so much as an Earth that can be habitable long ! In brief, all this Mammon-Gospel, of Supply-and-demand, competition, Laissez-faire, and Devil take the hindmost, begins to be one of the shabbiest Gospels ever preached, or altogether the shabbiest. . . ." (*Past and Present*. IX.) and so on, in a great smoke and fume shot with flame. But how splendidly a single image sometimes stands out ! "When the master of the horse rides abroad, many dogs in the village bark : but he pursues his journey all the same." (*Latter-Day Pamphlets*. IV.)

If Carlyle overbore his readers with a tremendous surge of words, John Ruskin (1819-1900), when he came to the stage of writing essays, adopted the simplest style in contrast with the purple passages which diversify his books—though these also can be quite simple when he wishes. His essays, which deserve the title since they are addressed to the common reader, are often on economic subjects, and were published in *The Cornhill Magazine* (1860) and *Fraser's Magazine* (1862-3). But the editors were so alarmed by the outcry raised by his mad economic ideas—he dared flout the established economists of his day—that they refused to go on printing them. ('Fraser's' was always pusillanimous and correct : it stopped Kingsley's *Yeast* half way through.) So Ruskin published his essays later as *Unto This Last* (1862) and *Munera Pulveris* (1872).

To us his ideas do not seem at all wild; many of them may now be found expressed in our statute books. He argued for a national system of education, for old age pensions, for a minimum wage, and paid the penalty of being too far ahead of his time, so far ahead that even now we have not caught up in every respect. Astonishing as it may seem, we have only latterly come, in any great numbers, to think what the following passage lays down :

"It is, therefore, the manner and issue of consumption which are the real tests of production. Production does not consist in things laboriously made, but in things serviceably consumable ; and the question for the nation is not how much labour it employs, but how much life it produces. For as consumption is the end and aim of production, so life is the end and aim of consumption." (*Unto This Last*. 77)

It is odd that Ruskin's passion for beauty should have led him to economics; but so it was. And his basic doctrine, we see, was not one of expediency, but of justice, and he developed this theme in admirable common-sense prose not without occasional glimpses of satire. His lectures on art can also be classed as essays.

We may think that the most important of this group, because his influence has been the most lasting, and the one to-day the most interesting because the matters he dealt with are still the subject of our aspirations and controversies, is Matthew Arnold (1822-1888). Carlyle hurled abuse at English society in the way we have seen ; Ruskin chided its neglect of

34

THOMAS BABINGTON MACAULAY (FULL FACE) WITH FRIENDS AND COLLEAGUES
IN THE HOUSE OF COMMONS, 1833
Detail from an oil painting by Sir George Hayter

beauty, and saw economics as the main barrier to its realisation ; Arnold
attacked its basic assumptions, its crass complacency. His attitude was the
opposite of Macaulay's, whom he regarded as the prophet of the Philistines.
Instead of the happy community which Macaulay saw spreading before
him, only a generation or two away from perfection, Arnold saw an aris-
tocracy impervious to ideas, a thick-skinned and vulgar middle class, and a
brutalised populace. For him England was made hideous by the Philistinism

35

(he introduced the word in its modern sense into our language) which constituted the attitude of those who embodied the culture of his time. His *Essays in Criticism*, published in 1865 and 1888, contained criticisms not only of literature, but also of the ideas behind literature, the ideas by which men live every day ; and he carried on the warfare in (besides many other books) *Culture and Anarchy* (1869), the amusingly satirical *Friendship's Garland* (1871), and in *Literature and Dogma* (1873).

His style is admirably flexible, persuasive, varied, and very clear ; indeed sometimes too clear. He is inclined to insist too much, especially in his later work, where he irritatingly repeats his favourite phrases, and seems to nag at you like the old-fashioned schoolmaster. One may in fact complain that, son of the famous headmaster Thomas Arnold, and himself an inspector of schools, he never quite divested himself of the gown, or let go of the dominie's fescue. But in the main he is charming, warm, always tolerant, never provincial ; and what is more important, he talks about matters which are still worth considering and taking to heart. Take for example, this extract from the first of his *Essays in Criticism I*, in which he has been arguing that the business of the critic is to encourage the free play of ideas, of the best ideas current at the time. Is it not as true now as it was then ?

"Do what he will, however, the critic will still remain exposed to frequent misunderstandings, and nowhere so much as in this country. For here people are particularly indisposed even to comprehend that without this free disinterested treatment of things, truth and the highest culture are out of the question. So immersed are they in practical life, so accustomed to take all their notions from this life and its processes, that they are apt to think that truth and culture themselves can be reached by the processes of this life, and that it is an impertinent singularity to think of reaching them in any other. 'We are all *terrae filii*' [sons of earth], cries their eloquent advocate ; 'all Philistines together.' Away with the notion of proceeding by any other course than the course dear to the Philistines ; let us have a social movement, let us organise and combine a party to pursue truth and new thought . . . and let us all stick to each other, and take each other up. Let us have no nonsense about independent criticism, and intellectual delicacy, and the few and the many. Don't let us trouble ourselves about foreign thought; we shall invent the whole thing for ourselves as we go along !"

Does that strike home at all ?

All his life Arnold tried to persuade people "to see the object as it really is" ; all his life he pleaded for "sweetness and light," for "the application of ideas to life," for grace, for manners, for spontaneity—all of which he called Hellenism ; as against the rigid morality, arid rules of conduct, which made the English Sunday of his day so grim an experience, which made life so drab—all of which he called Hebraism. And in this respect we can link him with Walter Pater (1839-1894), the great representative in this country of the aesthetic movement. Pater was not the lily-carrying, "greenery-

36

THOMAS CARLYLE, 1795-1881
Detail from an oil painting by Sir J. E. Millais

yallery, Grosvenor Gallery, foot-in-the-grave young man" he is sometimes supposed to be, no dreamy worshipper of beauty. What he directed his readers to was the increased vividness of life to be gained from being alert to beauty in all its forms ; and his Hellenism was no more a static worship of the past than Arnold's was. His best-known collection of essays is *Studies in the History of the Renaissance* (1873), and his most famous piece is the last in the book, which he at one time withdrew, lest it should misguide youth. It expresses his position quite clearly :

". . . The service of philosophy, of speculative culture, towards the human spirit, is to rouse, to startle it to a life of constant and eager observation. Every moment some form grows perfect in hand or face ; some tone on the hills or the sea is choicer than the rest ; some mood or passion or insight or intellectual excitement is irresistibly real and attractive to us for that moment only. . . .

"To burn always with this hard, gem-like flame, to maintain this ecstasy, is success in life. In a sense it might even be said that our failure is to form habits. . . .

"We are all under sentence of death but with a sort of indefinite reprieve. . . . we have an interval, and then our place knows us no more . . . our one chance lies in expanding that interval, in getting as many pulsations as possible into the given time. Great passions may give us this quickened sense of life, ecstasy and sorrow of love, the various forms of enthusiastic activity, disinterested or otherwise, which come naturally to many of us. Only be sure that it is passion—that it does yield you this fruit of a quickened, multiplied consciousness. Of such wisdom, the poetic passion, the desire for beauty, the love of art for its own sake, has most. For art comes to you proposing frankly to give nothing but the highest quality to your moments as they pass, and simply for those moments' sake."

This is the test Pater applied in his critical essays, full of solid thought, in *Appreciations with an Essay on Style* (1889), still fresh and worth reading; in *Greek Studies* (1895), and in

THE MONUMENT TO LYSIKRATES
Drawing from *The Antiquities of Athens*, 1825

38

WALTER PATER, 1839-1894
Lithograph by Sir William Rothenstein, 1894, from his *Oxford Characters*

the delightful *Imaginary Portraits* (1887), in which his own aim as a conscious stylist was best achieved. He is the only one of this group of essayists who was first and foremost a man of letters : it is only indirectly that he urges action to make life better. He is in no sense a reformer as the others were, but he offered his point of view with peculiar felicity, so that what he said had an appreciable effect on our manner of living.

Neither was Walter Bagehot (1826-1877) a reformer, and this brilliant much-neglected essayist belongs to this group rather by the accident of time than for any other reason. Yet he has something of the vehemence of the Victorian prophets, and like them spoke in a vigorous and no uncertain voice. He is more like Macaulay than any other writer, in his subjects, his

39

scale, his large digressions : but he is in many ways better than Macaulay—
if he has not quite his compelling, vivid, onrushing style—because he has
brilliant flashes of humorous wit, has a more incisive manner, and is not
so infuriatingly cock-sure. By profession a banker and shipping merchant,
he brought to his editorship of *The National Review* and *The Economist*
great literary qualities ; and he combined the sensibility, the intuition
of a man of letters with the practical philosophy of a City man. His intellectual interests were astonishingly wide. His *English Constitution* (1867),
his *Lombard Street* (1873) and especially his *Physics and Politics* (1872) are
classics in their kind, and eminently readable ; but his literary essays,
contributed chiefly to *The National Review* and published as *Literary
Studies* in 1879, are the works which give him his place here. His is a delightfully common-sense style, with common-sense wit ; he speaks, for
instance of Southey "who wrote poetry (as if anybody could) before breakfast" : he speaks to you as a sound man of affairs who knows what life is,
not without subtlety—since he knows that "mysticism is true"—and his
shafts hit the mark. "Among the disciples of Carlyle, it is considered that
having been a Puritan is the next best thing to having been in Germany."
One is always conscious of being spoken to by a man of hearty wisdom,
aware of the world, but open to other influences, based on wide reading.
How he differs from Macaulay can perhaps best be shown by his essay
on that historian (Jan. 1856), from which one can cull a few samples :

". . . Macaulay has exhibited many high attainments, many dazzling
talents, much singular and well-trained power ; but the quality which
would most strike the observers of the interior man is what may be called
his *in*experiencing nature. . . . His mind shows no trace of change. What
he is he was ; and what he was, he is. . . . He is so insensible to passing
objects, that they leave no distinctive mark, no intimate peculiar trace. . .

"He looks on a question [he says] as posterity will look on it ; he appeals
from this to future generations; he regards men as painful pre-requisites
of great-grand-children. . . .

"A great deal of this vividness Macaulay, of course, owes to his style.
Of its effectiveness there can be no doubt ; its agreeableness no one who
has just been reading it is likely to deny. Yet it has a defect. It is not as
Bishop Butler would have expressed it, such a style as is 'suitable to such
a being as man, in a world such as the present one.' It is too omniscient.
Everything is too plain. All is clear ; nothing is doubtful. . . ."

All this from an essay praising the *History*. Bagehot is always scrupul-
ously fair, well-balanced; a whole man is revealed behind his essays, never
trite but never extravagant ; always informative yet always genial (one
of his favourite words), aiming at generalisations, but always with his eye
on the object ; and however serious he may be, you never know when
the fun will not break out.

THE OLD AND THE YOUNG SELF : GILBERT KEITH CHESTERTON, 1874–1936
Water colour by Sir Max Beerbohm

THOMAS STEARNS ELIOT
Water colour by Katherina Wilczinski, 1946

THE end of last century and the beginning of this showed a decline in the force of the essay. It was no longer the mirror of the national mind ; it ceased to be tied to great issues. But in regaining its freedom it tended to become a toy rather than a vehicle of sturdy thought. Its writers seemed to look back to Lamb, and to look through a glass darkly. But men who have something to say will always manage to say it whatever form their time may force upon them; and Sir Max Beerbohm (b. 1872) is a triumphant example of the artist who, while seeming to be making only an exquisite plaything, is yet constructing an object of deeper value. His criticism took the form of delicious parodies, collected in *A Christmas Garland* (1912) ; but his more general musings on life are to be found in *And Even Now* (1922). His essays are fascinating because he surrenders to us a complete personality living in the world of his day ; rather a constricted world perhaps, but containing something that is common to all worlds. He is a descendant of Montaigne, and he offers us his being to delight in. We get it in glimpses. "It is a fact that not once in all my life have I gone out for a walk. I have been taken out for walks ; but that is another matter." Or when writing about laughter :

"Amidst the guffaws of a thousand strangers I become unnaturally grave. If these people were the entertainment, and I the audience, I should be sympathetic enough. But to be one of them is a position that drives me spiritually aloof. Also, there is to me something rather dreary in the notion of going anywhere for the specific purpose of being amused. I prefer that laughter shall take me unawares. Only so can it master and dissolve me. And in this respect, at any rate, I am not peculiar. In music halls and such places, you may hear loud laughter, but—not see silent laughter, not see strong men weak, helpless, suffering, gradually convalescent, dangerously relapsing. Laughter at its greatest and best is not there."

Fastidious, a little aloof, but humane and very human, Sir Max Beerbohm seems to bring with him the aroma of an age that is just past : his writings always were like that and they always will be ; just not quite up to date, and so, one guesses, enduring.

Gilbert Keith Chesterton (1874-1936) was always up to date ; whenever reading him one has the sense of battling valiantly in a present that badly needs shaking up. One sees the great burly figure, laughing in genial scorn at silly humanity which will not get things clear, fighting a fight for common sense and Catholicism. One may, perhaps, be now and again a little too conscious of religious propaganda; but there is so much liveliness in the thought, so much gaiety in the verbal play, such an abundance of happy sincerity, that even if one thinks differently from him one can forgive his having a design upon one. His style has not the classical neatness of Sir Max Beerbohm's ; it is sometimes Johnsonianly exuberant : but he makes his point, and leaves you, not musing as some essayists do, but actively thinking, combatively or not as the case may be. The punning, in ideas rather than in words, may sometimes irritate a little, but he puts us in such a mood that we can ever with a frolic welcome take the drizzle with the sunshine. Many will have read his essays in *The Illustrated London News*, or be familiar with the collections *All Things Considered* (1908), *Tremendous Trifles* (1909), *Generally Speaking* (1928), and *As I was Saying* (1936).

It is not true to say, as is often said, that Chesterton loved to deal in the paradoxical. What he did like doing was to take some accepted commonplace of the day, turn it inside out, and show how absurdly paradoxical it essentially was. He revelled in showing how we constantly confuse means with ends ; and all the time that he makes us chuckle he makes us think. This is not to say that he was always right—he would have hated to be thought the monster such a man must be—and his arguments are often lopsided, leading to wrong conclusions. But that does not matter ; he was basically sane, and it makes us saner to read him. The most remarkable thing about him is his sane patriotism.

The way he would leap from a seemingly trivial thing to one of obvious importance is admirably illustrated by his essay "On Maltreating Words." Beginning with a phrase picked out from a newspaper, which referred to "A Crusade to Reform Auction Bridge," he plunges into a splendid passage on the real crusades, "when the despair and darkness opened before the glory of Godfrey's ride ; when the toppling battle-towers swayed and sank in flames around the city as Godfrey leapt upon the wall . . ." He then goes on to talk about how the abuse of language creeps in :

"Somebody talks naturally enough about a crusade for liberty or a crusade for knowledge ; then the hunt is up and anybody who honestly believes in anything uses the term as a cliché; and we are all made familiar with the rush and hustle of a crusade for vaccination or against vivisection. In fact, the word 'crusade' begins by meaning 'movement' and ends with meaning merely 'proposal,' when it does not mean merely 'fuss.' We receive leaflets about a crusade against waste paper ; leaflets that are decidedly waste paper. We receive visitors with a crusade against muzzling dogs : visitors whom we ardently desire to muzzle. . . ." (*Generally Speaking.* xxiv.)

And so he goes on to other abuses of words, very entertainingly; then by a clever twist leads on to progress, and concludes with the Fall of Man. It is neat, it is brimful of life, and it leads you into paths you would probably be reluctant to tread but for his encouragement.

At present the essay, as a serious, yet personal, intimate, and friendly way of public utterance, is at a low ebb. Those who write 'easy' essays write idly about trifles, often with some elegance, in the tone of polite society ; but these things are essentially empty. The tendency is to write

"Un Revers"
Self-portrait in water colour by Sir Max Beerbohm

articles, not about things in general, about life as it is lived and thought about, or lived and not thought about except by the essayist, but about something in particular—literature let us say—from a rather expert or professional point of view. Of practitioners of this kind of art, Virginia Woolf (d. 1941) has in recent days been the most shining example. Giving her life to the solution of literary problems, especially in the realm of the novel, she was sensitive to the point of genius to every aspect of writing ; and, never conceiving it possible to divorce literature from life, she used an exquisite sensibility in making the public aware of the finer points of literature. Her essays, mostly contributed to *The Times Literary Supplement*, where, though anonymous, they were immediately recognisable because of the rhythmic quality of her unaffected style, were collected in *The Common Reader* (I. 1925, II. 1932), and were found to deal with a wide variety of literary figures and topics. Perhaps more than any other essays previously written, they invite the general public to enter into the secrets of, understand

43

the problems of, the artist who writes. Not that as a rule she tackles the subject directly : you pick up the ideas here and there as you read. She talks, so the title states, about Defoe, especially about *Robinson Crusoe* ; but what she is really discussing is the novelist's problem of spacing men, or Man, in relation to nature, and God. How much actuality do you want ? and how much spiritual reality ?—a question of perspective. What does Defoe do ?

He is going to tell us about a man on a desert island ; our imagination is filled, or prepared to be filled, with ideas of wild scenery, with thoughts on the nature of society, or on solitude and the soul. "We read," Mrs. Woolf says, "and we are rudely contradicted on every page. There are no sunsets and no sunrises ; there is no solitude and no soul. There is, on the contrary, staring us full in the face nothing but a large earthenware pot." She develops this delicately, entertainingly, flinching at nothing, till she sums up Defoe's astonishing achievement :

"Thus Defoe, by reiterating that nothing but a plain earthenware pot stands in the foreground, persuades us to see remote islands and the solitudes of the human soul. By believing fixedly in the solidity of the pot and its earthiness, he has subdued every other element to his design ; he has roped the whole universe into harmony. And is there any reason, we ask, as we shut the book, why the perspective that a plain earthenware pot exacts should not satisfy us as completely, once we grasp it, as man himself in all his sublimity standing against a background of broken mountains and tumbling oceans with stars flaming in the sky?" (*Common Reader*. II.)

With Virginia Woolf we are in the Montaigne part of the house ; her manner may be impersonal, but all the time we are asked to share the intimacy of her thought, the delicate quality of her personal apprehension. But there are very few who can write about literature for ever ; it is too much a part of life ; so that with the two essayists with whom this book will close we shall be concerned with men who have made literary essays the starting-point of what they have to say about life. With them the essay once more becomes more general, and with them we veer towards the Baconian apartments.

Thus we find that the first book of Thomas Stearns Eliot (b. 1888), *The Sacred Wood* (1920), is devoted entirely to literary subjects treated from the point of view of a man of letters ; but that his later ones, such as *For Lancelot Andrewes* (1928) aim rather at deriving philosophic or religious truths from what people have written, and to defining our attitude towards these writings : for "A man's theory of the place of poetry is not independent of his view of life in general." There is a certainty about Mr. Eliot's utterances which approaches the aphoristic (a matter of annoyance to those who hate making up their minds) ; yet the aphorisms are not thrown at you as axioms, being usually the conclusions of the arguments along which we have been led, in our close following of the subtle workings of a fastidiously

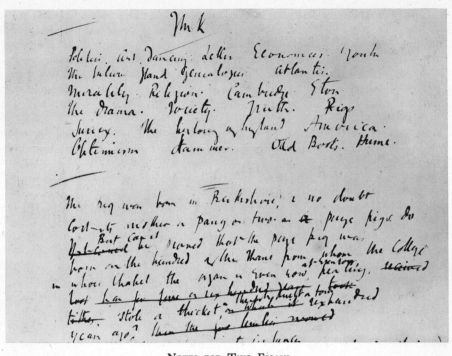

NOTES FOR TWO ESSAYS
Detail from a MS. book of Virginia Woolf

distinguishing mind. Here is an example from his essay on Matthew Arnold, with whom, in spite of wide divergencies, he has close affinities :

"We must remember that for Arnold, as for everyone else, 'poetry' meant a particular selection and order of poets. It meant, as for everyone else, the poetry that he liked, that he re-read ; when we come to the point of making a statement about poetry, it is the poetry that sticks in our minds that weights that statement. And at the same time we notice that Arnold has come to an opinion about poetry different from that of any of his predecessors. For Wordsworth and for Shelley poetry was a vehicle for one kind of philosophy or another, but the philosophy was something believed in. For Arnold the best poetry supersedes both religion and philosophy. I have tried to indicate the results of this conjuring trick elsewhere. ['Arnold and Pater' in *Selected Essays*.] The most generalised form of my own view is simply this : that nothing in this world or the next is a substitute for anything else ; and if you find that you must do without something, such as religious faith or philosophic belief, then you must just do without it. I can persuade myself, I find, that some of the things that I can hope to get

45

HERBERT READ
Red chalk drawing by Gregorio Prieto, 1943

are better worth having than some of the things I cannot get ; or I may hope to alter myself so as to want different things ; but I cannot persuade myself that it is the same desires that are satisfied, or that I have in effect the same thing under a different name." (*The Use of Poetry and the Use of Criticism*, 1933.)

Here, we may think, is the fusion of the Baconian method with that of Montaigne.

Tradition, one would say, is the rock upon which Mr. Eliot bases himself ; Mr. Herbert Read (b. 1893), on the other hand, finds an aid to his philosophy in the new instruments of human thought, such as psycho-analysis. Led along the philosophical and political road by considering the relation of literature and art to society—just as Ruskin and Morris were—and to the ideas dominating any society, he has widened the literary essay to include as much of life as he wishes. His *Collected Essays* (1938) may represent the ground covered in his earlier work, and *A Coat of Many Colours* (1945) reveals how his thoughts have ramified into the general sphere. He is Baconian, not so much in manner, as in the way in which he

46

always reaches out after some general truth, rather than, like Montaigne, inviting you to share his personal reactions. His style is that of a man telling you, familiarly enough, what conclusions he has come to, rather than that of one thinking aloud with you. His essay on Picasso's 'Guernica' picture shows both his manner, and how, with him, art leads to philosophic sociology :

"Art long ago ceased to be monumental. To be monumental, as the art of Michelangelo or Rubens was monumental, the age must have a sense of glory. The artist must have some faith in his fellow men, and some confidence in the civilisation to which he belongs. Such an attitude is not possible in the modern world—at least, not in our Western European world. We have lived through the greatest war in history [1914-18], but we find it celebrated in thousands of mean, false and essentially unheroic monuments. Ten million men killed, but no breath of inspiration from their dead bodies. Just a scramble for contracts and fees, and an unconcealed desire to make the most utilitarian use of the fruits of heroism."

Who can say that that is not addressed to 'the common reader' ?

CONCLUSION

IT is likely that essays will always be written, since the essay is the most adaptable of all forms : what they are like will depend upon two things, the means of publication and the reading public. So long as newspapers print essays—such as the last leading article in *The Times*—so long as weeklies continue, and monthlies and quarterlies, so long we shall get essays of appropriate length. It is the medium open for writers to use both when they have something to say and when they have nothing special to say. It is likely that essays will remain as diverse in intention and manner as they are now. When you have a homogeneous reading public and a restricted means of publishing, as you had in Queen Anne's day, then you will probably get essays all of one kind, as are those of Addison, Steele and their fellows : when you have a large and varied public, with papers and journals of all kinds, then you will probably get essays that are more and more specialised, more and more purposive. It is unlikely, then, that essays will ever again reflect a mood of society as a whole.

But we hope that there will always be people who want to be intelligently amused, who like to have a silent conversation by the fireside with a friendly person who does not make too great demands upon their mental activity, and who will, as he talks, bring to being a literary object which is in itself a delight. Sometimes such people will want a Bacon, sometimes a Montaigne ; so long as he is friendly, and so long as he knows what writing is, the man or woman who likes to spend a little leisure in reading will be satisfied.

Mrs. Rossetti Reading
Pencil drawing by Dante Gabriel Rossetti

SHORT BIBLIOGRAPHY

BOOKS ON ESSAYS AND ESSAYISTS

A Group of English Essayists of the Early Nineteenth Century, 1910, by C. T. Winchester. New York.—*The English Essay and Essayists*, 1915, by H. Walker. J. M. Dent.—*The Periodical Essayists of the Eighteenth Century*, 1923, by G. S. Marr. J. Clarke & Co.—*The Seventeenth Century English Essay*, 1926, by E. N. S. Thompson. Iowa

COLLECTIONS OF ESSAYS

Selected English Essays edited by W. Peacock.—*Critical Essays of the XVI to XVIII Centuries* edited by E. D. Jones.—*Critical Essays of the XIX Century* edited by E. D. Jones.—*Critical Essays of the XX Century*, edited by P. M. Jones.—all in World's Classics Series. Oxford University Press.—*Modern English Essays*, 1870-1920, edited by E. Rhys. Everyman Series. J. M. Dent.—*Nineteenth Century Essays*, 1912, edited by G. Sampson. Pitt Press Series.—*The English Familiar Essay*, 1916, by W. F. Bryan and R. S. Crane. Representative Texts. Boston